Severn River
Middle

Green Street 19.95 Summer 2002

ANDREW JOHNSON

Chris Hughes

BLACKBIRCH PRESS, INC.
WOODBRIDGE, CONNECTICUT

Published by Blackbirch Press, Inc.
260 Amity Road
Woodbridge, CT 06525
Web site: http://www.blackbirch.com
e-mail: staff@blackbirch.com

Printed in China

10 9 8 7 6 5 4 3 2 1

Photo credits:
Cover, pages 4, 16, 44, 83: (c)North Wind Picture Archives; cover (inset), pages 8, 18, 21, 24, 26, 28, 34, 43, 46, 57, 60, 61, 64, 65, 74, 75, 77, 78, 80, 82, 84, 86, 87, 90, 92, 99: The Library of Congress; page 6, 23: Blackbirch Press Archives; pages 10, 15: courtesy North Carolina Department of Cultural Resources Division of Archives & History, Archives and Records Section; pages 25, 33, 37, 42, 58, 66, 94: National Portrait Gallery; page 38: New York Public Library; page 79: National Archives.

Library of Congress Cataloging-in-Publication Data
Hughes, Christopher (Christopher A.), 1968–
Andrew Johnson / by Chris Hughes.
p. cm. — (The Civil War)
Includes index.
ISBN 1-56711-534-9 (alk. paper)
1. Johnson, Andrew, 1808–1875—Juvenile literature. 2. Presidents—United States—Biography—Juvenile literature. [1. Johnson, Andrew, 1808–1875. 2. Presidents.] I. Title. II. Civil War (Blackbirch Press)
E667.H84 2001
973.8'1'092—dc21 2001001703

CONTENTS

PREFACE: THE CIVIL WAR

Nearly 150 years after the final shots were fired, the Civil War remains one of the key events in U. S. history. The enormous loss of life alone makes it tragically unique: More Americans died in Civil War battles than in all other American wars combined. More Americans fell at the Battle of Gettysburg than during any battle in American military history. And, in one day at the Battle of Antietam, more Americans were killed and wounded than in any other day in American history.

Slaves did the backbreaking work on Southern plantations.

As tragic as the loss of life was, however, it is the principles over which the war was fought that make it uniquely American. Those beliefs—equality and freedom—are the foundation of American democracy, our basic rights. It was the bitter disagreement about the exact nature of those rights that drove our nation to its bloodiest war.

The disagreements grew in part from the differing economies of the North and South. The warm climate and wide-open areas of the Southern states were ideal for an economy based on agriculture. In the first half of the 19th century, the main cash crop was cotton, grown on large farms called plantations. Slaves, who were brought to the United States from Africa, were forced to do the backbreaking work of planting and harvesting cotton. They also provided the other labor necessary to keep plantations running. Slaves were bought and sold like property, and had been critical to the Southern economy since the first Africans came to America in 1619.

The suffering of African Americans under slavery is one of the great tragedies in American history. And the debate over whether the United States government had the right to forbid slavery—in both Southern states and in new territories—was a dispute that overshadowed the first 80 years of our history.

For many Northerners, the question of slavery was one of morality and not economics. Because the Northern economy was based on manufacturing rather than agriculture, there was little need for slave labor. The primary economic need of Northern states was a protective tax known as a tariff that would make imported goods more expensive than goods made in the North. Tariffs forced Southerners to buy Northern goods and made them economically dependent on the North, a fact that led to deep resentment among Southerners.

Economic control did not matter to the anti-slavery Northerners known as abolitionists. Their conflict with the South was over slavery. The idea that the federal government could outlaw slavery was perfectly reasonable. After all, abolitionists contended, our nation was founded on the idea that all people are created equal. How could slavery exist in such a country?

For the Southern states that joined the Confederacy, the freedom from unfair taxation and the right to make their

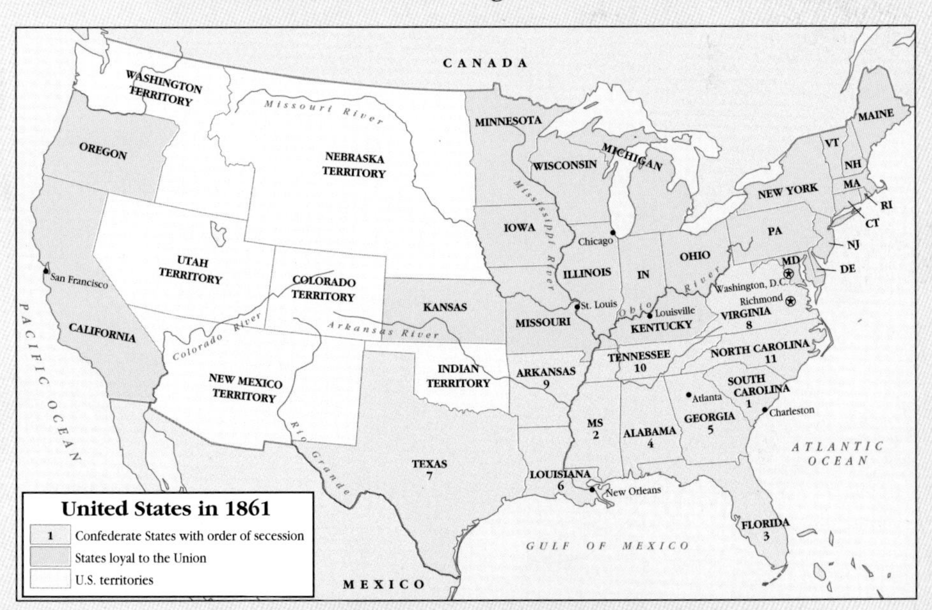

own decisions about slavery was as important a principle as equality. For most Southerners, the right of states to decide what is best for its citizens was the most important principle guaranteed in the Constitution.

The conflict over these principles generated sparks throughout the decades leading up to the Civil War. The importance of keeping an equal number of slave and free states in the Union became critical to Southern lawmakers in Congress in those years. In 1820, when Maine and Missouri sought admission to the Union, the question was settled by the Missouri Compromise: Maine was admitted as a free state, Missouri as a slave state, thus maintaining a balance in Congress. The compromise stated that all future territories north of the southern boundary of Missouri would enter the Union as free states, those south of it would be slave states.

In 1854, however, the Kansas-Nebraska Act set the stage for the Civil War. That act repealed the Missouri Compromise and, by declaring that the question of slavery should be decided by residents of the territory, set off a rush of pro- and anti-slavery settlers to the new land. Violence between the two sides began almost immediately and soon "Bleeding Kansas" became a tragic chapter in our nation's story.

With Lincoln's election on an anti-slavery platform in 1860, the disagreement over the power of the federal government reached its breaking point. In early 1861, South Carolina became the first state to secede from the Union, followed by Mississippi, Florida, Alabama, Georgia, Louisiana, Virginia, Texas, North Carolina, Tennessee, and Arkansas. Those eleven states became the Confederate States of America. Confederate troops fired the first shots of the Civil War at Fort Sumter, South Carolina, on April 12, 1861. Those shots began a four-year war in which thousands of Americans—Northerners and Southerners—would give, in President Lincoln's words, "the last full measure of devotion."

OPPOSITE: The Confederate attack on Fort Sumter began the Civil War.

INTRODUCTION: THE LINE IS DRAWN

★ ★ ★ ★ ★

Andrew Johnson became president in 1865.

In the 1860s, the train ride from Washington D.C. to Greeneville in eastern Tennessee was a bone-rattling journey across the Blue Ridge Mountains that lasted several days. As a member of the House of Representatives and as a Senator, Andrew Johnson had made the trip home to his family in Greeneville many times. However, this trip—in late April 1861—would be unlike any he had ever taken.

Johnson was going home a few weeks after the first shots of the Civil War had been fired at Fort Sumter, South Carolina. He planned to speak out against Tennessee's secession across his state. Eleven Southern states had left or would soon leave the Union to form the Confederate States of America. Members of Congress from Southern states had left Washington to take up the cause of the Confederacy. Among them was Johnson's fellow Senator, Jefferson Davis of Mississippi, who had become the president of the Confederate States.

Johnson was a Southerner from a Southern state. He owned several slaves. As loyal as he was to Tennessee and to Southern political views, Johnson was more loyal to the Union—and he was unafraid to say so on the Senate floor. Now, at station after station in Tennessee, the Senator saw straw-filled dummies bearing his likeness hung in effigy. Then, as the train arrived at one stop, a crowd gathered on the platform. Some cursed Johnson and called him a traitor. Others in the crowd entered the train. One man held a hangman's noose as the group bullied its way toward Johnson's car.

Andrew Johnson, a man who had held public office in Tennessee from more than thirty years, now faced a lynch mob. The time for discussing differences had passed—Johnson pulled a pistol from his coat and aimed it at the mob. Pulling back the hammer of the gun, he warned his fellow citizens to turn around or be shot. The train was soon on its way, but a line had been drawn—the Civil War had come to east Tennessee.

Chapter 1

THE TAILOR'S APPRENTICE

Raleigh, North Carolina, was not a large or wealthy city in 1808. There were some exclusive areas where a small number of rich citizens lived, but most people in Raleigh had little to do with those areas. The city also had sections in which needy families struggled to survive. It was in one of those poor sections and into one of those needy families that Andrew Johnson was born on December 29, the youngest of three children. Though he would eventually become a congressman, a senator, a governor, a vice president, and America's seventeenth president, there was little about Andrew Johnson's birth or childhood that marked him for success.

OPPOSITE: Andrew Johnson was born in this house in Raleigh, North Carolina.

★

About two months after Johnson's birth, Abraham Lincoln was in a log cabin in Kentucky.

★

Andrew's father, Jacob Johnson, was a bank janitor, and his mother, Mary, worked as a weaver to bring in extra money—something that was always needed. Despite his poverty, Jacob Johnson was known in the Raleigh community as a hard worker and an honest man.

One day, when Andrew was three years old, Jacob saw a boat capsize on a pond. The three men on board began to sink as Jacob jumped into the water. He managed to drag all three safely to shore, but the incident made Jacob Johnson ill. Soon, weakened by illness, the elder Johnson died. A newspaper editor in Raleigh wrote an article about the death, and praised Andrew's father:

> *Died, in this city on Saturday last, Jacob Johnson, who for many years occupied a humble but useful station . . . he was esteemed [respected] for his honesty, sobriety, industry, and his humane, friendly disposition.*

The editor had good reason to praise Jacob Johnson—he was one of the men Jacob had pulled from the pond. Andrew's sister had died in childhood, so his mother Mary was left to raise Andrew and his older brother, William, alone.

There were no public schools in Raleigh at the time, and the Johnson family had no money for private school. The only education the Johnson brothers received came from running around Raleigh's dirt-covered streets. Then, in 1818, when William was fourteen and Andrew was ten, they were taken in as apprentices for a local tailor named James Selby.

Learning a trade was not an unusual step in those days for boys unable to attend private school. The boys' small income helped to feed the family, which by then included Mary's new husband, Thomas Doughtry.

Andrew quickly discovered that the tailor's shop was more than a place to make and mend clothes. Selby's shop was a gathering place for wealthy citizens, local politicians, and public speakers. People came to the shop to read books and articles aloud and to debate political issues.

★

As a young slave, Frederick Douglass learned to read by using *The Columbian Orator*.

★

Here, young Andrew listened to the speakers and discussed their ideas with his brother and his friends at the shop. Some local men noticed Andrew's interest in politics and debate. One man gave him a copy of a book of speeches, *The Columbian Orator*, which Andrew particularly liked. He had already memorized some speeches from hearing them recited, and eventually, the foreman at Selby's taught Andrew basic reading and writing, so the young man could continue learning on his own.

As much as they enjoyed learning, however, the Johnson brothers were also full of mischief. One day, as a prank, teenaged Andrew; his brother, William; and two friends threw stones at the home of an unfriendly neighbor. She threatened to sue, and the boys decided to run away. Mr. Selby, unhappy about losing the services of the two apprentices he had spent years training, offered a reward for Andrew and William. He posted a notice in the paper that read:

> *Ran away. . . two apprentice boys, legally bound, named William and Andrew Johnson . . . I will pay the above reward ($10) to any person who will deliver said apprentices to me in Raleigh, or I will give the above reward for Andrew Johnson alone.*

★

In 1824, the year Andrew Johnson ran away, Thomas "Stonewall" Jackson was born in Northern Virginia.

★

The boys fled fifty miles away to Carthage, North Carolina, where Andrew found work as a tailor. Since they could be returned as long as they stayed in North Carolina, however, they eventually crossed into South Carolina and settled in a town called Laurens, where no one knew them.

Andrew stayed in Laurens for almost two years, working in a tailor's shop and falling in love with a girl named Mary Wood. When Johnson asked her to marry him, Mary's mother refused to allow her daughter to marry a poor tailor with a questionable past and a doubtful future. Saddened, Andrew decided leave South Carolina.

Realizing that he had to return to Raleigh to clear his name, Andrew visited Selby to settle any debts that he owed the older man for his

Ten Dollars Reward.

RAN AWAY from the Subscriber, on the night of the 15th instant, two apprentice boys, legally bound, named WILLIAM and ANDREW JOHNSON The former is of a dark complexion, black hair, eyes, and habits. They are much of a height, about 5 feet 4 or 5 inches The latter is very fleshy, freckled face, light hair, and fair complexion. They went off with two other apprentices, advertised by Messrs Wm. & Chas. Fowler When they went away, they were well clad—blue cloth coats, light colored homespun coats, and new hats, the maker's name in the crown of the hats, is Theodore Clark. I will pay the above Reward to any person who will deliver said apprentices to me in Raleigh, or I will give the above Reward for Andrew Johnson alone.

All persons are cautioned against harboring or employing said apprentices, on pain of being prosecuted.

JAMES J. SELBY, Tailor.

Raleigh, N. C. June 24, 1824 26 3t

In 1824, ten dollars was more than two weeks' salary for the average working person.

training. By then Selby had sold his tailoring business and retired a wealthy man, but he was still angry with the boys for leaving town after their prank. He said that Andrew and William owed him an extra fee for running away. Andrew, who had very little money, decided he had no choice but to leave North Carolina once again.

VOTE
FOR
OLD
HICKORY
NEW ORLEANS
HENRY CLAY
COUNTY COURT
ANDY JACKSON
FOR EVER
PATRIOTS
ADVANCE!

Chapter 2

BUSINESSMAN AND POLITICIAN

In 1825, seventeen-year-old Andrew traveled to Tennessee, relying upon strangers for occasional meals and wagon rides. When he reached Knoxville, on the Tennessee River, he rode a flatboat south to Decatur, Alabama. Andrew had no real plans, he simply followed rumors of job opportunities. In Alabama, he worked as a tailor. When he became restless again, he walked north to Columbia, Tennessee, and took a job with a tailor named James Shelton. After several months, he tried to return to Raleigh, but his problems with Selby had not improved. Finally, Andrew packed up his mother and stepfather, put their belongings in an old cart pulled by a pony, and moved his family to Tennessee for good.

OPPOSITE: Andrew Jackson, a Tennessee pioneer who became the seventh president, would become Andrew's political idol.

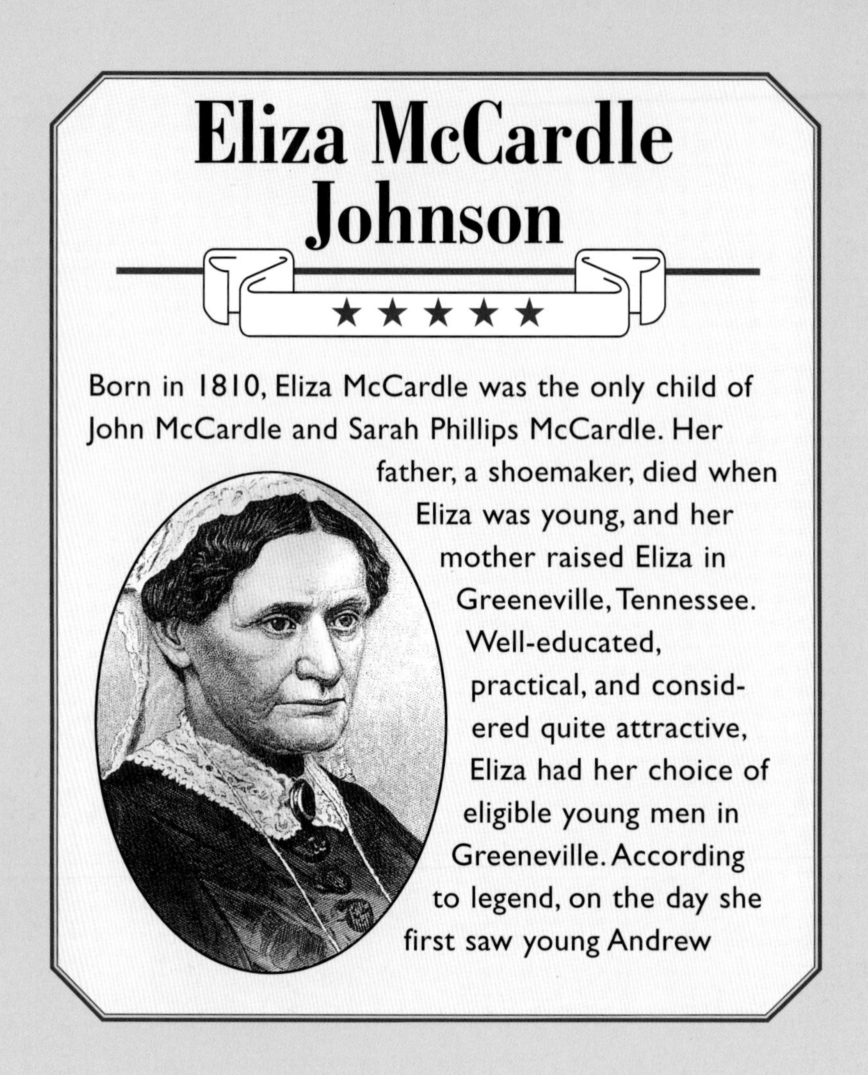

Eliza McCardle Johnson

★ ★ ★ ★ ★

Born in 1810, Eliza McCardle was the only child of John McCardle and Sarah Phillips McCardle. Her father, a shoemaker, died when Eliza was young, and her mother raised Eliza in Greeneville, Tennessee. Well-educated, practical, and considered quite attractive, Eliza had her choice of eligible young men in Greeneville. According to legend, on the day she first saw young Andrew

Their long journey ended in the small town of Greeneville, in eastern Tennessee. There, Johnson learned that the town's tailor was planning to retire. This convinced him to settle in Greeneville, where he rented rooms for his family and began to work. A businessman at seventeen years old,

Johnson, she turned to her friends and said, "There goes the man I am going to marry." In 1827, the two were indeed married, by Mordecai Lincoln, a distant cousin of the eventual president.

Eliza taught Johnson to write and do some math, and she often read to him as he worked in his tailor shop. Once Andrew began his national political career, Eliza spent most of her time in Greeneville raising their five children. That time was seldom easy. In middle age, she developed "consumption," a term for tuberculosis or other lung diseases, which would make her an invalid for most of her life. She was harassed and abused by Confederates during the Civil War. She joined Andrew briefly in Nashville when he was a military governor, and again in Washington when he became president, though most of the duties as hostess she left to their daughter, Martha.

Eliza died on January 15, 1876, only six months after Andrew's death. She was buried next to him in Greeneville.

Andrew quickly began to meet townspeople. Among his first acquaintances was Eliza McCardle, the daughter of a shoemaker.

Andrew was immediately drawn to Eliza by her looks—and by her intelligence. Though she was the daughter of a working man, Eliza could read, write, and solve math problems. In a young country such as the United States, where the first college for women would not open its doors until 1836, Eliza's education was very unusual. Only fifty years earlier, at the beginning of the American Revolution, fewer than half of the women in the colonies could write their names.

In the spring of 1827, when Andrew was eighteen and Eliza sixteen, the two were married. It was a union that would last nearly fifty years. Eliza spent her first years as a newlywed polishing Andrew's spotty education. Though he already knew the basics of reading, she improved his skills while teaching him spelling, composition, and math.

★
In 1827, abolitionist John Brown owned a successful leather tannery in western Pennsylvania.
★

The young couple lived in the back of a house they rented in Greeneville, and Andrew opened his first tailor shop in the front. Andrew soon proved himself a smart businessman. Following his wife's advice, he bought another shop as well as other property in Greeneville. His family expanded with his business and investments. In 1828, Andrew and Eliza had a daughter named Martha. In 1830 came a son, Charles. Next came Mary in 1832, and Robert in 1834. Many years later, in 1852, Eliza bore Andrew, Jr. who was called Frank.

Public Life

As his business and land holdings grew, Johnson became active in Greeneville politics. Inspired by

the political discussions he had once listened to at Selby's shop, he read books on political topics—or had Eliza read while he worked. Johnson's interest in politics came at a time of great change in the American political system. In the early years of the country's history, voting in most states was limited to white men who owned property. Generally, this put voting power in the hands of wealthy landowners and kept it out of the hands the working class, a group known as "common" men.

Most property requirements were declared illegal by the 1820s. For the most part, however, the men elected to office came from the class of

The first six presidents, including Thomas Jefferson, were wealthy landowners.

wealthiest Americans. In fact, whether from the North or South, the first six presidents of the United States were wealthy property owners.

Like many people of his time, Johnson believed that for a democracy to work, the voices of all citizens should be heard. And he wasn't afraid to make his opinions known about the rights of the "common" man around Greeneville.

Johnson began debating in public and discovered he had a talent for arguing his point of view. In 1829, Andrew Johnson, portraying himself the voice of the working man, was elected alderman—a town official. Johnson was just twenty-one, old enough to vote legally for the first time, when he was elected to his first public office. He was re-elected in 1830 and became Greeneville's mayor in 1834. Those were the first of many elections Johnson would win over the next forty-five years.

★

Jackson had a scar on his cheek, the result of being slashed as a child during the Revolution by a British officer when he refused to polish the "Redcoat's" boots.

★

Johnson's success was helped by another Tennesseean who was elected to the presidency. In 1829, Andrew Jackson became the president of the United States. He was the first "people's president"—a man who had come from poor beginnings and become a voice for the "common" man. A military hero in the War of 1812, Jackson's inauguration brought huge crowds of his admirers from the western frontier to see "Old Hickory" sworn in. So many of his admirers showed up at the White House to shake

Jackson's hand that the new president had to sneak out an office window to avoid being crushed by the mob.

Andrew Jackson, a hero in the War of 1812, became the seventh president and the first president from the "frontier."

Johnson, who came from the same roots as the president, became a follower of Jackson's politics. Some of Jackson's views would guide the tailor from Greeneville for the rest of his life. As the popularity of Jackson's "common" man politics rose, Johnson followed those policies and decided to run for the state legislature in Nashville, the capital. Both of his opponents were more experienced and more widely known in the district. Using his great speaking skills, however, Johnson defeated both men so completely in a debate that one dropped out of the race. In October, he was elected easily and continued his public career as a state representative.

At this point, Johnson was still forming his political views, and he was sometimes caught between his support for the Democrats of President Jackson and the new Whig Party. The Whigs took their name from a British political party that had

Martin Van Buren, the eighth president, was in office when the U.S. suffered an economic depression.

struggled against their king. Many Whigs felt that Jackson had used his power as president almost like a king, weakening large banks and fighting legislation that aided large businesses. Some Whigs even referred to Jackson as "King Andrew." Jackson told his critics that he was only standing up for the common man, against laws that made "the rich richer and the potent more powerful."

Johnson's strong connection to Jackson and to the working class as well as his opposition to using tax dollars to build railroads and aid "big business", brought him into conflict with the Whigs. Johnson felt that railroad owners received too many favors from the federal government and were using tax dollars to make themselves even wealthier. He voted to keep railroads from laying tracks through Tennessee.

Many people in Johnson's district, however, favored railroads for speedy travel and ease in transporting goods from farms to large markets. His opposition to railroads made Johnson unpopular, and he was defeated for re-election in 1837. This was one of only two times in Johnson's long political career that he would lose a popular election. Still popular enough in Greeneville to return to his position as mayor, Johnson had now developed a taste for higher office. In 1839, he confirmed his loyalty to the Democratic Party and was re-elected to the state legislature.

Back in Nashville again, Johnson used his position to increase his popularity across the state. His talent as a speaker drew large crowds. One observer described Johnson's speech as "forcible and powerful, without being eloquent. He held his crowd spell-bound. There was always in his speeches more or less wit, humor, and anecdote."

William Henry Harrison, the ninth president, died after only two months in office.

During the 1840 presidential campaign, Johnson made a

William "Parson" Brownlow

Beginning in 1840, Andrew Johnson's career was tied to the fiery and outspoken Parson Brownlow. Born in 1805, Brownlow was orphaned at an early age. At various points in his life he was a carpenter, a preacher, an editor, an author, and a politician. He was pro-slavery, but violently anti-secessionist. In 1840, he began to oppose Andrew Johnson. He thought Johnson was "an unmitigated liar . . . and a villainous coward." For the first part of Johnson's career,

number of speeches in favor of the re-election of Democratic President Martin Van Buren. Van Buren was running against the Whig candidate, William Henry Harrison.

In the course of the campaign, Johnson came into conflict with William G. "Parson" Brownlow, a man who would play a large role in his political life from then on. Parson Brownlow was a

Brownlow constantly attacked him in his newspaper, *The Whig*, which became the largest weekly paper in the South in the 1850s.

The Civil War changed the relationship between Johnson and Brownlow, who began to praise Johnson's strong stand for the Union, and, for a time, became Johnson's strongest supporter. Brownlow, known as the "fighting parson," was forced out of Tennessee by the Confederates but returned when Johnson became military governor. He helped nominate Johnson for the vice-presidency in 1864.

After the Civil War, however, Brownlow turned on Johnson again. The parson sided with the Radical Republicans, and went into politics to push his ideas. He was governor of Tennessee from 1865 until 1869, then elected to the Senate in 1869. He served there until 1875, when he was replaced by Andrew Johnson. Brownlow died in 1877.

minister and a newspaper editor who became Johnson's main political enemy for several years.

In 1840, Brownlow labeled Johnson a "toady," one who tries to please people on both sides of an issue. Despite Brownlow's attacks and Van Buren's loss to Harrison, Johnson's reputation was so strong that he was elected as a state senator in 1841.

Chapter 3

CONGRESSMAN AND GOVERNOR

By 1841, Johnson, thirty-three years old, had completely devoted himself to politics. He had built a successful tailoring business, hiring several other employees in his shop. Eventually, he sold his business and focused on politics and his profitable real estate deals. Among other properties, Johnson now owned a large house across from the tailor shop, as well as a farm where his mother and stepfather lived. He also owned several slaves. He never sold any of the slaves that he bought, but he had no objection to owning them.

OPPOSITE: The Capitol Building in Washington, D.C. was expanded during Andrew Johnson's terms there.

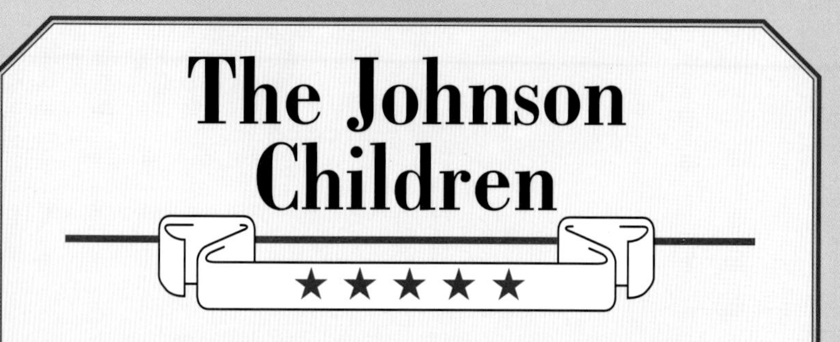

The Johnson Children

Andrew and Eliza Johnson had five children. Martha, the oldest, married David T. Patterson, a lawyer and judge who served as a U. S. Senator for Tennessee after the Civil War. Martha became the official hostess of the White House during her father's presidency and won widespread praise. Martha and David had two children, Andrew Johnson Patterson and Mary Belle Patterson. Martha died in 1891.

Charles was the second child. Alcoholism marked most of his adult life. A strong Unionist like his father,

As with many other Americans at the time, Johnson's racial prejudice was deeply rooted. In Johnson's view, the "black race of Africa were inferior to the white man in point of intellect—better calculated in physical structure to undergo drudgery and hardship."

By 1843, because of a change in the boundaries of voting districts, it became possible for a Democrat to be elected to Congress, and he served in the Union army for a time as a surgeon. In 1863, he was killed in a fall from his horse.

Mary, the third child, married Dan Stover in 1852. They had three children: Lillie, Sarah, and Andrew Johnson Stover. Like Patterson, Dan Stover was a loyal Unionist who served as a colonel during the Civil War until his death in 1864. Later, Mary married William R. Brown, but the two were divorced after Andrew Johnson's death. Mary died in 1883.

Robert was the fourth child. For a while, he appeared to be following his father into politics, but, like his brother, alcohol undid him. After several bouts with depression, Robert killed himself in 1869.

Andrew, Jr. (called Frank) became a journalist, but was in poor health for much of his life. He died in 1879 at the age of 27.

Johnson wanted that post. Again, he was strongly opposed by Parson Brownlow, who called Johnson a "villainous blackguard, and low bred scoundrel, with . . . characteristic baseness, malice, and coarse language."

Despite such attacks, which were common in the rough politics of the time, Johnson won election to the U.S. House of Representatives. He would go on to win five consecutive two-year terms in Congress, spending the next decade serving in Washington.

As much as he loved his wife and young family, Johnson went to Washington alone. The capital was still being built, and the humid climate and muddy streets made it an unpleasant place to live at certain times of year. Most Congressmen in those days left their families at home and lived in rented rooms.

In addition, Eliza was not in good health. She had developed "consumption," a term used at that time for tuberculosis and for any lung disease that caused a person to become an invalid. Johnson and his wife both decided that she should remain in Tennessee with their children while he went to Washington.

As a representative, Johnson generally voted in favor of limiting the size and expense of government programs. At the same time, however, he favored expansion of the United States by adding the Texas territory as a state. Johnson also spoke out against any abolition of slavery. He viewed slaves as property and, like many Southerners, believed the Constitution guaranteed the right to own property.

In 1844, Johnson supported Tennessee Democrat James Polk for president against Whig candidate Henry Clay. Although Johnson did not agree with Polk on all issues, he did agree with Polk's stand on admitting Texas into the Union. Southern lawmakers in general also favored Texas statehood.

Many Southerners felt that Texas was large enough to be divided into several pro-slavery states. For the same reason, the North opposed the addition. With strong Southern support, however, Polk won the presidency in 1844. The following year, Texas was added to the Union on the condition that it not be divided into more than four states.

★
In 1844, Jefferson Davis, who would lead the confederacy, was elected to the House as a representative from Mississippi.
★

Johnson returned home in 1845 to run again for Congress and again defeated his old nemesis, Parson Brownlow. During Johnson's second term in Washington, he voted in support of a war with Mexico. The war had been brewing since Texas had gained its independence from Mexico in 1838. For several years, the state had been an independent country of Americans. The disagreement over Texas' border with Mexico helped bring the U.S. into a war.

James K. Polk of Tennessee became president in 1844, and led the U.S. into the Mexican War.

At the Battle of Vera Cruz, the Mexican army was defeated by U.S. forces under General Winfield Scott. Here, Scott accepts the surrender of Mexican leaders.

The war also resulted from the idea of Manifest Destiny. During the 1840s, many Americans believed strongly in this point of view, which held that the United States was a unique democracy and had the special right to occupy the entire continent. Acting on this

attitude meant, for example, removing Native Americans from their traditional lands so white Americans could settle there.

In 1845, Manifest Destiny led the U.S. to annex—or add—Texas to the Union. Mexico considered this an act of war. When Mexico objected to the southern border of the new state, many Americans felt that Mexico should be taught a lesson. Some even went so far as to suggest that the country become part of the United States.

★

In 1845, the autobiography of escaped slave Frederick Douglass became a best-selling book in the North.

★

Johnson was a vocal supporter of President Polk's efforts. At the same time, however, he angered his own supporters by voting against a pay raise for soldiers, against the establishment of the Smithsonian Institution, and against establishing a federal prison system. All of these, he argued, would cost the "common" man money.

In 1846, Johnson took one of his most controversial political positions when he introduced the Homestead Bill, which would allow a person to claim 160 acres of public land in western territories at very little cost. Ownership of the land would be given to a settler if he lived on it for five years and made improvements to it.

The Homestead Bill was unpopular with many Southerners because they felt the western land was not likely to be settled by slave owners. Such a bill, they claimed, would add several non-slave states to the Union as people moved west. Though his bill was voted down in 1846, Johnson made it his personal goal to see it pass eventually.

Over the next few years, Johnson continued to carve his unique political path. At certain times, he supported the Democrats and the South, but other times he opposed them. Johnson's political beliefs were not entirely shaped by his Southern roots,

however. They were also shaped by his roots as a "common" man—a self-taught tailor who had never been to school. These roots brought him into conflict with wealthy slave-holding landowners on some issues.

Slave holder and war hero Zachary Taylor became president in 1848.

Though he faced close elections, Johnson was sent to Washington in 1847, 1849, and 1851. In those years, he pushed his Homestead Bill, still without success. He also acted in favor of the veto power of the president and in favor of religious tolerance.

Johnson also worked for changes in the U.S. electoral system. He voted to have presidents elected directly by the people, rather than by the Electoral College. He was also in favor of direct election of senators, who were elected by state legislators at that time. Neither bill passed, and it wasn't until 1913 that senators were directly elected.

In 1848, Zachary Taylor, a Whig and a hero of the Mexican War, was elected president. Taylor

Nashville, the capital of Tennessee, was a growing city in the early 1850s, when Johnson was governor.

owned more than 300 slaves and had great support in the South. Johnson had supported Democrat Lewis Cass, who was also a Southerner, but had no strong feelings about slavery. Taylor had won both in Tennessee and across the nation.

The question of slavery was creating deep divisions across the country, and despite the fact that Johnson supported slavery at every opportunity, many Southerners did not trust him. They resented his support for homesteading and his opposition to Taylor.

In 1852, Johnson was finally able to pass his Homestead Bill in the House, only to see it defeated in the Senate. That same year, Democrat Franklin Pierce was elected president. The Whigs,

however, won power in Tennessee's government. They were able to re-draw the boundaries of voting districts to make sure that there weren't enough Democrats in Johnson's new district to re-elect him.

Governor Johnson

Knowing that new voting boundaries would keep him from office, Johnson did not run for Congress in 1853. Instead, he ran for election as governor of Tennessee. Opposed by Whigs and by many Democrats who did not trust him, Johnson used his popularity with the working class to help his cause. His political skills as a dealmaker also served him well. He promised important political positions to various Whigs, which helped him win the election over Gustavus Henry. One local newspaper stated,

★
In 1852, Harriet Beecher Stowe's antislavery novel *Uncle Tom's Cabin* was published. By 1853, more than 300,000 copies had been sold.
★

Johnson has gained a great triumph in Tennessee. He has beat Henry, the Whig party, as well as a large part of the leaders of the Democratic party. The masses have done the work, the mechanic, the day laborer, have in this election, come to the rescue.

The position of governor in 1853 was not powerful, but Johnson used it to his advantage. He spread his "common man" ideas and worked to build his personal popularity. He continued to speak proudly of his humble background, tailoring his own clothes, and even sent a suit he made to the governor of Kentucky.

Still living without his family, who remained in Greeneville, Johnson was able to achieve significant victories as governor. He helped create a state system of public schools, a state library, and supported various programs for agriculture including an Agriculture Bureau and a regular agricultural state fair. In 1855, he won re-election against an anti-Catholic and anti-immigrant party called the Know-Nothings.

Johnson's devotion to his political career, however, cost him a great deal in his personal life. Living most of the year in Washington or Nashville, he was often absent from family events, and his children and grandchildren saw little of him.

During his second term as governor, Johnson was kept busy in the state capital at Nashville. Because travel during this era was difficult and time-consuming, his duties kept him away from his family, several hundred miles east. His daughter, Martha, was married without her father present, and Johnson missed the birth of his first grandchild to his daughter, Mary. Also, while he was away, his mother died. His son, Charles was sinking into an alcohol addiction. Robert, who appeared headed for politics, was troubled by poor health. Eliza's health was also a growing concern, especially as she cared for the baby, Frank.

Toward the end of his second term as governor, Johnson decided to run for U.S. Senator. He had helped the Democrats achieve strength again in Tennessee by supporting the presidency of James Buchanan. Johnson had briefly considered running for president in 1856, but was convinced he did not have enough support. Instead, he focused on the Senate seat and was elected in 1857.

★

In 1856, abolitionist John Brown led a raid on pro-slavery settlers, killing five men in "Bleeding Kansas".

★

Senator Johnson

Becoming a Senator was a remarkable achievement for a man from such humble beginnings. Johnson now belonged to one of the most powerful bodies in the nation at a time of bitter division. The United States was quickly moving

James Buchanan was the fifteenth president.

toward a split between the North and the South, and Johnson's Southern loyalty would often clash with his firm belief in the Union.

Johnson's first order of business in the Senate was re-introducing his Homestead Bill. Again opposed by Southern states, the bill was finally amended and passed in 1860, only to then have President Buchanan veto it. It finally passed and was signed into law by President Lincoln in 1862, partly as a reward for Johnson's loyalty to the Union cause.

Johnson made a number of speeches defending both slavery and the Union. His goal in taking these two opposing positions was the presidential election of 1860. Johnson felt he would be a good compromise candidate. His views on slavery had Southern support, his homesteading bill had Northern support, and his Unionism appealed to moderates on both sides.

Like Johnson, Abraham Lincoln came from humble beginnings.

To his disappointment, the Democratic nomination in 1860 went to Stephen Douglas, with the Southern Democrats splitting off to support John Breckenridge. The weakened Whig

This banner appeared at a South Carolina convention after secession.

party nominated John Bell. A newly formed anti-slavery party, the Republicans, nominated Abraham Lincoln.

The two Democratic candidates took votes from each other, which allowed the Republican candidate to win. In 1860, Abraham Lincoln became the sixteenth president with just 39 percent of the popular vote, one of the lowest percentages in U.S. history. With Lincoln's election on an anti-slavery platform, many Southerners felt that their rights—and their way of life—were about to be taken from them. Even though many Southerners did not own slaves, most felt that the right of states to make their own decisions regarding slavery, taxation, and other issues was guaranteed by the Tenth Amendment to the U.S. Constitution. Led by South Carolina, several states voted to secede—or withdraw—from the Union. They planned to form their own nation.

Johnson, a Southerner, was strongly opposed to breaking up the Union. Asked what he would do with secessionists, Johnson replied, "I would have them arrested and tried for treason, and, if convicted . . . they should suffer the penalty of the law at the hands of the executioner."

Tennessee had many strong Union supporters, but it was mainly a slave state with stronger ties to the South than to the North. Johnson would soon have a hard fight on his hands and a life-changing decision in front of him.

Chapter 4

DEFENDER OF THE UNION

On December 18, 1860, Senator Johnson rose from his Senate seat to declare his position. He spoke over the course of two days, declaring his firm commitment to the Union and his belief that states did not have the right to secede. He also maintained that the government had the right to protect its property and defend itself against treason. In other words, Johnson supported the use of force to keep states in the Union. He ended his long speech with a strong declaration of his anti-secession ideas.

OPPOSITE: Union Army recruits near Chattanooga, Tennessee.

I will not give up on this Government . . . . I intend to stand by it, and I entreat every man throughout the nation who is a patriot . . . to rally around the altar of our common country . . . and swear by our God, and all that is sacred and holy, that the Constitution shall be saved, and the Union preserved.

Johnson's speech had a tremendous impact. Southerners, including many from his own state, felt betrayed. For them, the South—with its unique culture and way of life—was more of a "nation" than all the states together. Johnson was calling on the government to forcefully prevent the states from seceding. Most Democrats agreed with Southerners. Northerners, Republicans, and Whigs praised Johnson's words. Even his bitter enemy, Parson Brownlow, came to Johnson's defense. Newspapers, such as *The New York Times* and *The Chicago Tribune*, praised the speech. Even Johnson's opponents admitted the speech was both powerful and influential. Alexander Stephens, who became the vice president of the Confederacy, described the speech as:

One of the most notable, as it was certainly one of the most effective, ever delivered by any man on any occasion. I know of no instance in history when one speech effected such results . . . . It did more to strengthen and arouse the . . . people at the North than everything else combined. The author stood . . . isolated from every public man throughout the Southern states.

A fellow Senator simply stated that Johnson's speech "caused the Civil War."

Johnson Loses Tennessee

At first, the impact of the speech in Tennessee was great. It helped Unionists in the state legislature vote down the governor's call for a convention to discuss secession. In April, however, when the Civil War began with the attack on Fort Sumter in South Carolina, Tennessee secessionists called for a new convention. Johnson left Washington to fight for the Union in speeches across Tennessee. He was often harassed, taunted, and even threatened by his enemies. On June 8, 1861, Tennessee voted to secede from the Union, though Johnson's own region of Greeneville and east Tennessee voted with the Senator.

★
At the beginning of the Civil War, Ulysses Grant was working as a clerk in his father's hardware store in Illinois. Within three years, he would command all Union forces.
★

Suddenly, Johnson's freedom and his life were in danger as Confederate troops moved into the state. His former enemy, Parson Brownlow, received a letter that showed the danger Unionists faced in Tennessee: "The South can look upon you in no other light than as a traitor and the twin brother of Andrew Johnson. Remember, and beware, you shall be hung in the year 1861."

Johnson, who opposed Lincoln and the Republicans in the 1860 election, now became one of the president's strongest supporters. As Lincoln took drastic steps to increase his power, Johnson

made speeches defending him. Johnson was now even more heroic to people in the North. The Republicans began to see him as a valuable friend, while the Democrats lost faith in him. President Lincoln praised "the conspicuous examples of devoted loyalty from . . . Andrew Johnson of Tennessee . . . giving [his] whole soul and strength for the cause of the Union."

★

A little more than one month after Tennessee seceded from the Union, the first major battle of the war was fought at the Bull Run River in Manassas, Virginia.

★

At the same time he was receiving praise for his Unionist stand, Johnson co-sponsored the Johnson-Crittenden Resolution, which stated that the war was being fought only to defend the Union, and that it should end as soon as that goal was achieved. Johnson supported the act because he did not want the war to be used to further punish the South or to end slavery.

Johnson used his popularity to try to help Unionists in eastern Tennessee. He promised that he would not go home unless accompanied by a Union army, and several states offered to serve as his temporary home until that happened. Instead, Johnson traveled through Kentucky and Ohio, trying to persuade military leaders there to rescue Tennessee from the Confederacy. At the same time, Tennessee Unionists were in real danger. Parson Brownlow was arrested and sent North. Johnson's son Robert had to go into hiding, and his son Charles was taken to court. One son-in-law was arrested, the other joined a guerrilla army against the Confederates. Worst of all, Johnson's invalid

Tennessee in the Civil War

The state of Tennessee was in a difficult position in the Civil War. Though it was a slave state, it did not rely on slave labor as much as its Southern neighbors did. Many people in Tennessee had ties to the North, and there were strong Unionist feelings throughout the state when the war began. Though the secessionists won in 1861, many parts of Tennessee continued to resist the Confederates.

Because it was on the border of the Union, President Lincoln was particularly interested in winning Tennessee back. After several failed attempts to find a general who would succeed in taking Tennessee, Ulysses S. Grant finally achieved success in 1862. With victories at Forts Henry and Donelson in February, Grant opened the door for Andrew Johnson's appointment as military governor.

Johnson's time as military governor was marked by strife and discord. Confederates constantly threatened to return in force, and even Unionists disagreed about how to reform the government. Finally, after his election as vice-president, Johnson was able to return a full civilian government to his state. Tennessee was readmitted to the Union in 1866.

Severn River Media Center

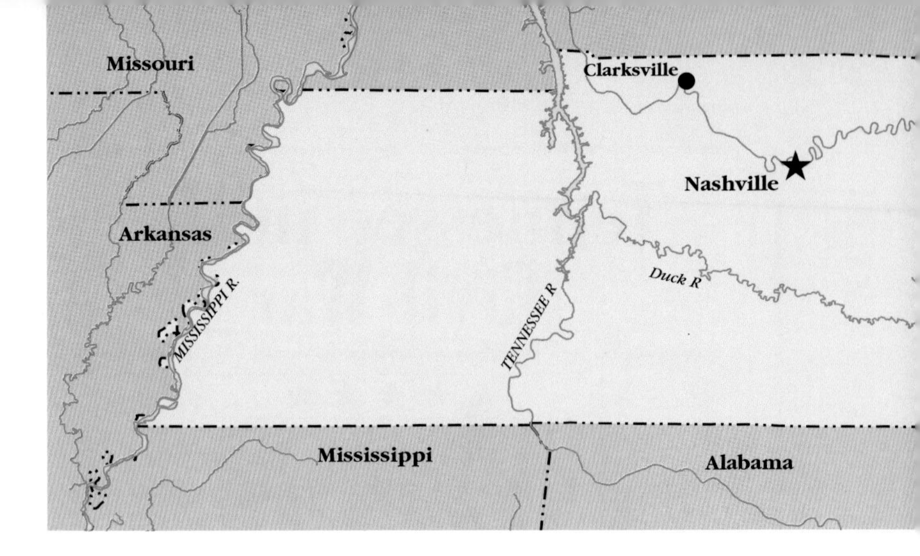

wife and young son were constantly harassed. Eventually, they had to move in with his daughter Mary when Johnson's property was taken and used as a Confederate army hospital.

When Johnson's efforts to force a Tennessee invasion failed, he returned to Washington late in 1861. There, he met with President Lincoln and the newly appointed Commander of the Union forces, General George McClellan, both of whom agreed with his desire to free east Tennessee.

Because of his popularity and his active involvement, Johnson was appointed to the Joint Committee on the Conduct of the War, a group of mostly Republican Senators and Congressmen who tried to encourage Union generals to take action. In part because of pressure from this group, Northern forces began to push harder and slowly gained victories in the West. In January 1862, a Union victory at Mill Springs in Kentucky eventually led to the Union to take control of Cumberland Gap at the edge of east Tennessee. At the same time, other Union forces threatened the city of Chattanooga.

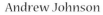

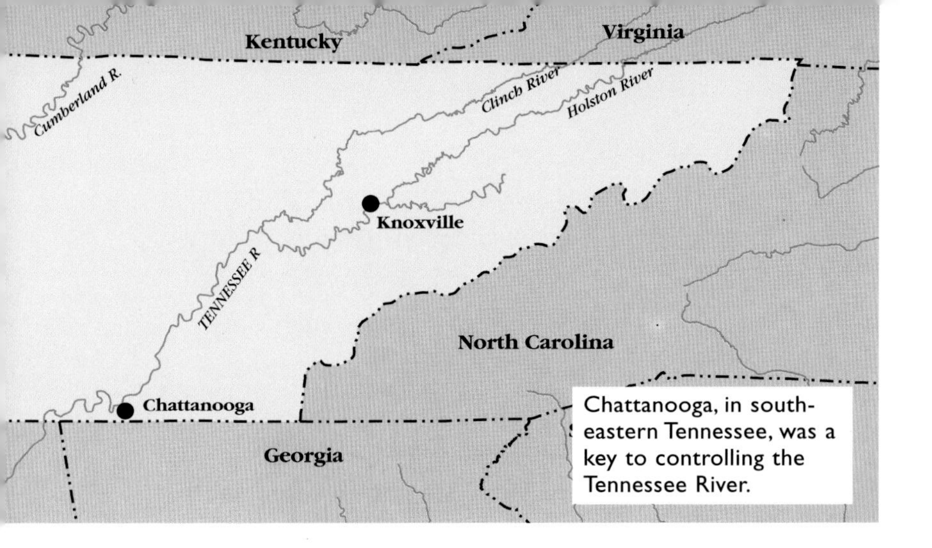

Chattanooga, in southeastern Tennessee, was a key to controlling the Tennessee River.

These attacks opened the door for Union victories at Fort Henry and Fort Donelson in northern Tennessee for forces commanded by General Ulysses S. Grant. The Confederates evacuated Nashville and much of central and western Tennessee, though they stayed in force in the eastern part of the state.

Military Governor

The events in 1862 gave Lincoln the chance to pull Tennessee back into the Union, but he needed someone to reorganize its government, push out the Rebels, and defend the Unionists. Lincoln realized immediately that the best person for the job was Johnson. On March 4, Johnson was appointed military governor of Tennessee. The choice was popular, and Johnson's fellow Senators unanimously confirmed him. He was also given the military rank of brigadier general.

Johnson's duty was to re-establish order in Tennessee, and rebuild the government. As he described it in an early speech:

I have been appointed . . . as military governor for the time being, to preserve the public property of the State, to give the protection of law. . . and, as speedily as may be, to restore her government to the same condition as before the existing rebellion."

His appointment, however, was not popular with everyone in Tennessee, where he had been called an "alien enemy of the people," as well as a traitor by the Confederates and even some pro-Union Democrats. One military leader wrote Johnson a warning before the new governor reached Nashville. "You must not expect to be received with enthusiasm, rather the reverse, and I would suggest you enter without any display." The Confederate governor, who fled to Mississippi, tried to increase distrust of Johnson by saying, "If Andy Johnson were a snake, he would hide in the grass and bite the heels of rich men's children."

Even those who wanted to rejoin the Union were divided into two main groups. One group, mainly Democrats, wanted to protect slavery and mend relations with the South. The other group, largely Republicans and old Whigs, wanted to end slavery and punish the Rebels. Johnson's natural sympathy was with the first group, but he knew that most of his support came from the second group, and so he tried to create a middle position between the two. It was a position that would become increasingly difficult as the war continued.

In his first speech from Nashville, he said, "I return to you with no hostile purpose. I come with the olive branch [symbol of peace] in one hand and the Constitution in the other." In the same speech, however, Johnson also stated that traitors must be punished and treason crushed.

In fact, Johnson could not do much in Tennessee because large parts of the state were still in Confederate control. Though the Union won a victory at Shiloh in April 1862, that battle pulled Union forces west and left Nashville undefended. Soon Confederate forces were threatening the capital. Governor Johnson stood firm. "Andy Johnson says if the rebels retake Nashville, they will find his remains under the ruin of the Capitol," as one newspaper reported. And more than once Johnson threatened to shoot anyone who talked of surrender. He also pledged to destroy secessionist homes and burn the city before he would let it fall.

In the parts of Tennessee he controlled, Johnson required people to take oaths of allegiance to the United States. He closed newspapers that were pro-Confederate. He imprisoned Rebel leaders and anyone in a public position—including ministers—who refused to take the oath. These acts violated citizen's rights, but Johnson believed they were needed to save the Constitution. In fact, he was not as tough on Confederates as he claimed. Many of those who spoke out against the Union were quickly released from jail or never arrested.

★
The Battle of Shiloh was called the Battle of Pittsburg Landing by Union forces, who were commanded in Tennessee and the West by U. S. Grant.
★

During this time, Johnson's family was a source of anxiety and sadness to him. Eliza was able to leave east Tennessee with Frank, Charles, and Mary's family to join Johnson in Nashville. Eliza was still unwell, however, and Mary soon took her to Indiana. Robert—who was in the army near Cumberland Gap—and Charles had both become addicted to alcohol. Martha remained in Confederate-controlled Greeneville. Then, in April 1863, Charles was killed in a fall from a horse.

★
In May 1863, Confederate General Stonewall Jackson was mistakenly shot by his own troops during the Battle of Chancellorsville, Virginia. He died ten days later.
★

Despite his personal worries, Johnson was mainly concerned with his role in bringing the two sides back together. The most challenging question for him to address was slavery. He still defended the institution, believing that African Americans were inferior to whites. As time passed, however, a new idea began to enter his speeches. He realized that slavery was the main issue dividing the two sides, and he knew that defending the government was more important than defending slavery. To Confederates, he said, "If you persist in forcing the issue of slavery against the Government, I say in the face of Heaven, 'Give me my Government and let the negroes go!'"

At this point, Lincoln had also reached a crossroads. In September 1862, Lincoln issued his Emancipation Proclamation, which freed all slaves in territories still under rebellion as of January 1, 1863. Governor Johnson was able to convince

In the spring of 1863, Union General Grant ordered military training for freed slaves. Those freedmen later fought for the Union at Vicksburg.

Lincoln that Tennessee did not qualify as a state "in rebellion" and should be protected from the law. This earned Johnson praise from Tennessee's slaveholders. Still, Johnson knew which way the nation was heading.

In early 1863, Johnson toured some Northern states on his way to Washington, which confirmed his popularity as the hero of Tennessee, and opened his eyes to political possibilities. The presidential election of 1864 was approaching, and Johnson saw himself as a possible candidate. He realized he would need the support of Republicans who opposed slavery, as well as that of his fellow Democrats, many of whom opposed him. This realization brought him to a final decision on the slavery question. Declaring that slavery was "a cancer on our society," Johnson called for full emancipation, or freedom, for slaves. He even began to raise a military force of African American troops in Tennessee.

Chapter 5

TRAGIC PRESIDENT

By 1864, Union military victories had made President Lincoln popular, and Johnson decided against challenging him for the presidency. As it turned out, Lincoln, had his own plan for the Tennessee governor. His vice-president, Hannibal Hamlin, was a Radical Republican from Maine. Lincoln already had the support of the Republicans, and Hamlin did not add to that support. He wanted a joint party made up of all Unionists from both parties. To win, Lincoln knew he needed a vice-president who could bring in votes from a different party and a different region.

OPPOSITE: Johnson replaced Hamlin as vice-president in 1865.

Johnson was the perfect choice. As Lincoln's secretary wrote, "Mr. Johnson . . . was not only a Democrat, but also a citizen of a border slave-holding state, and had rendered distinguished service to the Union cause." At the National Union Party convention, Johnson's old enemy-turned-friend, Parson Brownlow, raised Johnson's name.

We have a man down there whom it has been my good luck and bad fortune to fight untiringly and perseveringly for the last twenty-five years—Andrew Johnson. For the first time . . . three years ago we got together on the same platform, and we are fighting the devil and [Confederate president] Jeff Davis side by side!

Hannibal Hamlin served as vice-president during Lincoln's first term.

After much discussion, the new Union party unanimously approved the Lincoln-Johnson ticket.

In the election, Lincoln and Johnson faced Democrats General George McClellan and George Pendleton. Fortunately for Lincoln, the Union army's pursuit of Rebel forces through the South, following the major blow to Confederate forces at Gettysburg, disproved McClellan's claim that Lincoln could not win the war. When the final vote was counted, the Union party had defeated the Democratic ticket in almost every state, including Tennessee. Andrew Johnson was returning to Washington.

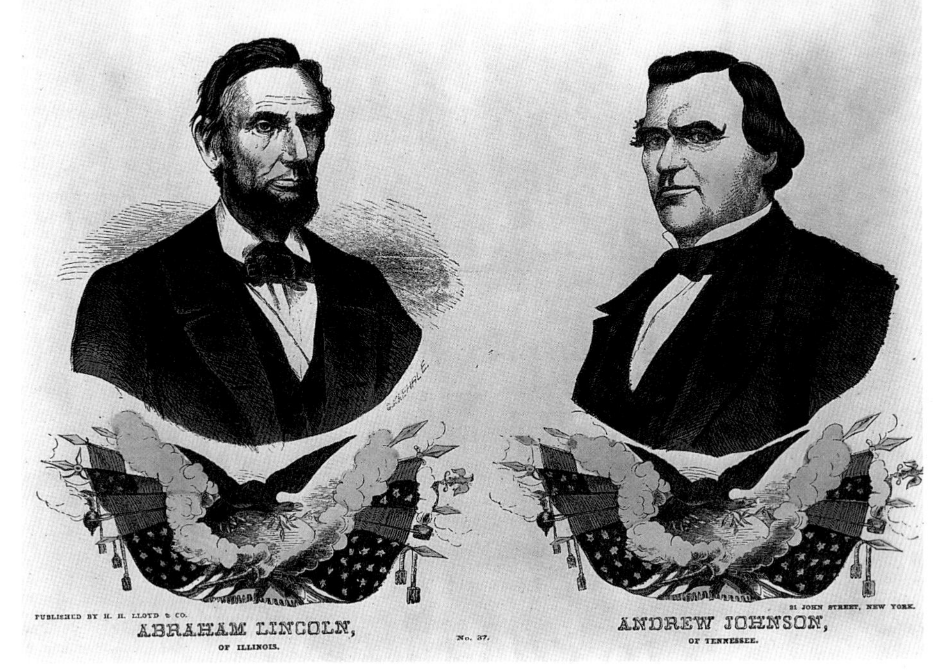

PUBLISHED BY H. H. LLOYD & CO.
ABRAHAM LINCOLN,
OF ILLINOIS.
No. 37.
21 JOHN STREET, NEW YORK.
ANDREW JOHNSON,
OF TENNESSEE.

The Lincoln-Johnson ticket swept to victory in the election of 1864.

As military governor, Johnson's performance had been notably mixed. He had not been able to restore the government of Tennessee completely, and, while in power, he had trampled many Constitutional rights he valued. On the other hand, he had kept Confederates from regaining power and had protected Union supply lines and railroads.

Vice President

Early in 1865, Johnson came down with typhoid fever, which left him tremendously weakened. On his way to the inauguration in Washington, traveling, as usual, without his family, the illness continued to trouble him. The night before the inauguration, Johnson joined a friend in drinking several glasses of whiskey. The next day, just before the ceremony, he had three more glasses of whiskey "to steady himself." The result was obvious to everyone gathered there to see Lincoln and Johnson sworn into office. Andrew Johnson attended his own inauguration thoroughly drunk.

★ Words from Lincoln's second Inaugural Address are inscribed on the walls of the Lincoln Memorial in Washington, D.C. ★

Considered one of the best public speakers of his time, Johnson gave a speech that was so unclear and hard to follow that witnesses immediately recognized the problem. Though Lincoln's speech, which followed, was considered among his greatest, the day had been ruined by Johnson's behavior.

Democrats ridiculed Johnson and Republicans hung their heads in shame. The newspaper accounts ranged from humor to fury. Several called on the new vice-president to resign. *The New York World* wrote, "To see the vice-presidency defiled by this insolent, drunken brute . . . and to think that one frail life stands between this insolent, clownish creature and the presidency! May God bless and spare Abraham Lincoln." In the official report on the inauguration written by President Lincoln's secretaries, there is not a single mention of the vice-president.

Lincoln stood by Johnson, even as demands came in for the vice-president's resignation. As he said, "I have known Andy Johnson for many years; he made a bad slip the other day, but you need not be scared; Andy ain't a drunkard."

In fact, Johnson did drink, and both of his sons suffered from alcoholism, but this is the only time in his long career that he was ever noticeably drunk in public. Unfortunately, the accusation would stay with Johnson until long after his death.

Once the humiliation of the inauguration was past, the government had work to do. In early April, Richmond fell to the Union, and on April 9, Confederate General Robert E. Lee surrendered his army to Union General Ulysses S. Grant at Appomattox Court House in Virginia. The Civil War was virtually over. Johnson, who had recovered from his illness—if not from his embarrassment—made a few public speeches calling for punishment—even death—for leading Rebels. On Good Friday, April 14, he went to President Lincoln to convince the president not to be too easy on the Confederate leaders. It was their first meeting since the inauguration disaster, and would be Johnson's last conversation with Lincoln.

Lincoln Assassinated

That night, at Ford's Theater in Washington, actor John Wilkes Booth shot President Lincoln in the head. Andrew Johnson had gone to bed early that night, and he was awakened by a loud knock at the door at 10:15 P.M. Told of the shooting, Johnson went to the house where Lincoln lay dying, then returned to his hotel. Word began to come in that the assassination plot went beyond Lincoln. Secretary of State William Seward had been attacked in his home and severely wounded

On the night of Lincoln's assassination, George Atzerodt had been assigned to kill Johnson.

by Booth's associate Lewis Paine, who also stabbed Seward's son, an army doctor, and several other people. Later, it was learned that another member of the plot, George Atzerodt, had been ordered to assassinate Johnson at his hotel that night, but he had lost his nerve.

Strangely, Booth had come to see Johnson on the morning of the assassination. Finding the vice-president away, Booth left his calling card at Johnson's hotel. In case Johnson was not killed, Booth hoped his calling card might throw suspicion on Johnson.

By 7:30 the next morning, Lincoln was dead. Supreme Court Chief Justice Salmon P. Chase came to Johnson's hotel to give him the Oath of Office, and Andrew Johnson officially became America's seventeenth president.

The New President

The tailor from Tennessee was in a tough position. He was suddenly faced with running a nation in shock and mourning. First, Booth and his compatriots had to be caught and punished. Then came the huge responsibility of reuniting a nation divided by war. In his first speech as president, Johnson said:

I feel incompetent to perform duties so important and responsible as those which have been so unexpectedly thrown upon me . . . My past public life, which has been long and laborious, has been founded . . . upon a great principle of right, which lies at the basis of all things.

Though he had supported Lincoln in many areas since 1861, Johnson had his own ideas about the war and about how to lead the nation's recovery. Some Radical Republicans violently disagreed with Lincoln's plan to accept Rebels back into the Union. They liked Johnson because he talked frequently of punishing the Rebels. One Radical Republican, Senator Benjamin Wade, said, "Johnson, we have faith in you. By the gods, there will be no trouble now in running the Government."

Johnson took the Oath of Office on the morning of April 15, 1865.

Secretary of State William Seward was stabbed the night of the Lincoln assassination.

Wade and his colleagues thought Johnson was a Radical, but they soon realized their error. In fact, Johnson's real views on the South were much softer than his public statements. He believed that certain individuals could be punished as traitors, but the states as a whole should not suffer as a result of the rebellion. This was consistent with the Johnson-Crittenden Resolution passed early in the war.

Republicans had a different view. They wanted to make sure that the South was weakened after the war so the North could continue to control the government. Most Republicans also wanted to permanently guarantee the end of slavery, and they wanted to protect the rights of the freed slaves, especially in the South. Congress had passed the Thirteenth Amendment to the Constitution ending slavery and now it was up to the states to ratify it.

One of Johnson's first major decisions as president was choosing his advisors. Lincoln's cabinet was a mix of radical and conservative leaders who disagreed in their visions for reconstructing the South. Johnson decided to keep Lincoln's cabinet intact to give people confidence in the government after America's first presidential assassination. Secretary of State William Seward, injured on the night of the assassination, led the cabinet. Edwin Stanton remained as secretary of war, and would cause trouble for Johnson. Other important Cabinet members included Navy Secretary Gideon Welles, Treasury Secretary Hugh McCulloch, and Attorney General James Speed. Of these, Seward and Welles became Johnson's strongest supporters.

Lincoln's widow, Mary, was bedridden with grief for more than a month after the assassination, and Johnson decided not to move into the White House right away. Instead, he rented a house in the city and held his meetings at the Treasury Department. When he did move into the presidential residence, he decided to finally bring his family together in Washington. By June, Eliza and Martha had moved into the White House with him. Eliza's continued illness, however, forced Martha to serve as official hostess for most events.

Presidential Reconstruction

Johnson did not make any unpopular moves in the early months of his term. His kindness to Mrs. Lincoln and willingness to retain Lincoln's cabinet earned him praise. In addition, his immediate moves to punish Lincoln's assassins met with widespread approval. Booth was killed during his capture, but several associates, including Paine and Atzerodt, were caught. After a military trial, four men were hanged and four others were sentenced to prison.

By this time, Confederate President Jefferson Davis had been captured by Union calvary, effectively ending the Civil War. The question of how to handle the South could not be avoided. Johnson believed that, as president, managing the so-called "reconstruction" was his task. Many lawmakers, especially Radical Republicans, thought that it was Congress's right to create and enforce the policies in areas that had seceded.

★

The Civil War did not truly end until April 26, 1865, when Confederate General Joe Johnston surrendered to Union General William T. Sherman.

★

Because Congress was not in session when Johnson began the process, however, he had the chance to establish his own Reconstruction program without interference. He decided to be lenient with the states, following the statements Lincoln had made before his death. On May 29, 1865, President Johnson issued the following proclamation:

> *I hereby grant to all persons who have, directly or indirectly, participated in the existing rebellion . . . amnesty and pardon, with restoration of all rights of property, except as to slaves . . . upon the condition, nevertheless, that every such person shall take and subscribe the following oath . . .*

The oath was a statement of loyalty to the government and the Constitution, but not all Confederates were offered this pardon. Johnson excluded certain groups from his offer, including former Confederate government officials, high-ranking officers, anyone who left Congress or a judicial position to join the South, governors in seceded states, anyone who had mistreated Union prisoners, and any Confederate with taxable property over $20,000. Johnson did allow anyone in these categories to apply for a pardon, however, and he promised pardons would be easily gained. Johnson also declared that only people who had taken loyalty oath could hold office, and that voting rights would be exactly as they were before the war.

★

Radical Republicans planned to arrest Robert E. Lee for treason until General Grant threatened to resign if his old enemy was arrested.

★

Radical Republicans were furious. They claimed Johnson's acts were illegal because the Constitution did not give the president these powers. More importantly, they objected to the ease with which former Rebels regained power, and the fact that Johnson made no effort to protect freed slaves.

In fact, Johnson strongly recommended to provisional governors he appointed that they ratify the Thirteenth Amendment, refuse to pay any debt they had assumed under rebellion, and formally withdraw their acts of secession. He even recommended giving the vote to certain freedmen who were literate and owned property. However, his refusal to legally require any of these steps infuriated the Radicals. Congressman Thaddeus Stevens wrote to Senator Charles

Sumner, "Is there no way to arrest the insane course of the president in Washington?"

★
In 1856, Senator Charles Sumner was nearly beaten to death on the Senate floor by a South Carolina lawmaker who objected to Sumner's anti-slavery statements.
★

The South was quick to accept Johnson's generous terms. Most states followed at least some of his recommendations of revoking secession, giving up their debts, and ratifying the Thirteenth Amendment. They did not, however, follow his recommendation to give voting rights to former slaves. In fact, Southern legislatures did just the opposite. Most Southern states passed "Black Codes" that specifically denied African Americans the rights to vote, serve on juries, testify in court against a white person, marry a white person, or earn equal pay to whites. These codes effectively returned freedmen to almost the same condition as slavery.

Northerners who hoped to see African Americans gain rights were horrified at the result of Johnson's plan. By December 1865, most Southern states were ready to return to the Union, but they had paid almost no penalty for their rebellion. When Johnson declared that land in the South had to be returned to all pre-war white owners, despite the fact that many freedmen had farmed and developed some of that land, the Radicals leaped into action.

War with Congress

Johnson's decisions about Reconstruction were based on three main ideas. He wanted to restore pre-war conditions as quickly as possible. He did

The Freedmen's Bureau

Six weeks before his assassination, President Lincoln established the Freedmen's Bureau. This government agency was created to help war refugees get their farms working again. It was also given the responsibility of helping freed slaves—called freedmen, whether they were men, women, or children—start a new life.

The Freedmen's Bureau played an important role in the South after the war. Agency workers handed out millions of free meals to black and white refugees. The Bureau built hospitals and treated sick African Americans. It also helped freedmen find jobs and protected them against the unfair restrictions set out in the Black Codes.

One of the most important tasks of the Freedmen's Bureau was building schools and sending teachers to the South to give African Americans the education that had been denied them. Under the Bureau, four colleges were set up in the South, and more than 250,000 children went to school for the first time.

The Freedmen's Bureau Bill, passed by Congress in 1866, continued funding this agency. Most lawmakers felt that Andrew Johnson would sign the bill, but the bill also gave the bureau power to decide legal matters regarding civil rights. Johnson believed those matters were for local courts and vetoed the bill. His veto was overturned.

★

Frederick Douglass met with Johnson to ask him to speak out against the "Black Codes."

★

not think the states should have to go through any major ordeal to regain their status as states. Second, he was still in favor of states rights, and believed that the Tenth Amendment to the Constitution guaranteed each state the right to pass its own voting laws, property laws, and any other rights not assigned to the federal government. Finally, Johnson did not believe that freedmen should be given power in the South. There were a large number of African Americans in the South, and Johnson feared that allowing them to vote could give them real political power—and perhaps even allow some to be elected to office.

Still controlled by his prejudiced views of race, Johnson was quoted as saying, "This is a country for white men, and, by God, as long as I am president, it shall be a government for white men."

When Congress returned to session, the Radical Republicans gained support for their own Reconstruction plans from their more moderate colleagues. Lawmakers passed a bill extending the funding for the Freedmen's Bureau, an agency that had been created to help freed slaves gain rights and protection in the South.

Johnson used his power to veto, or deny, the bill's passage. Part of his reason was that the South was not represented in Congress when the act was approved. His refusal to compromise with Congress, however, gained him a large number political enemies. Soon, those who opposed the president were in the majority in Congress, and could use their power to defeat his plans. When Southern states held elections and sent representatives to Washington, Congress refused to recognize their legality.

In March 1866, Congress passed a Civil Rights Bill. This law gave citizenship to anyone born in the United States, and guaranteed certain rights and protections to all citizens including the "full and equal benefit of all laws and proceedings for the security of person and property as is enjoyed by white citizens." The act also gave control of civil rights cases to federal courts rather than state courts.

This act went against much of what Johnson believed was needed to bring the South back into the Union. In a long response, he vetoed this bill, claiming it was passed without Southern representation. Johnson also wrote that the act gave African Americans "safeguards which go infinitely beyond any that the General Government has ever provided for the white race."

This time, however, Congress was ready for the veto. The Constitution allows Congress to overturn a presidential veto if two-thirds of both Houses vote for it. On April 6, 1866, Johnson's veto was overturned and the Civil Rights Act became law.

Such back-and-forth actions began a new period in relations between Johnson and Congress, a period marked by battles that

★

Johnson was the first president to travel the country giving speeches to influence public opinion and gain support.

★

After the 1866 passage of the Civil Rights Bill, many African American men in the south voted for the first time.

showed how bitter divisions between North and South still remained. Over the next two years, Johnson vetoed a total of twenty-nine congressional bills. Fifteen of those vetoes were overturned as Congress took complete control over Reconstruction.

Congress passed another version of the Freedmen's Bureau over Johnson's veto, and an act giving African Americans the right to vote in Washington, D.C. It also passed the Fourteenth Amendment, which guaranteed many of the rights from the Civil Rights Act to all citizens and barred Confederate leaders from political office.

Perhaps the most important action taken by Congress during that time occurred in 1867, when lawmakers established a new system of Reconstruction, again passed over Johnson's veto. This plan called for the South to be divided into five military districts, each headed by a general who would reorganize local politics and make decisions in the regions. The harsh requirements placed on the South were meant to punish the rebels and keep their leaders from any high office. This plan completely overruled Johnson's own Reconstruction acts, but there was little he could do about it.

Northerners who went to the South to take over regional governments were called "carpetbaggers" by Southerners.

Northerners who traveled South to take over regional governments were called "carpetbaggers," a name taken from the fashionable luggage they brought. Those Southerners who worked with Northerners were known as "scalawags." Both groups were despised by the Southerners they controlled.

The Fourteenth Amendment

In passing the Fourteenth Amendment, Northern lawmakers set out the terms for Southern states to rejoin the Union. Some historians consider it the most important amendment to the Constitution, other than the Bill of Rights.

The first section of the amendment defines a citizen of the United States as anyone born or naturalized in the country. It then gives all citizens rights that cannot be taken without "due process of law," as well as guaranteeing all citizens "equal protection under the law." This section gave African Americans the benefits and protections given to other American citizens.

The second section declares that a state's representation in Congress can be reduced if it denies the right to vote to any adult male citizens.

The third section forbid anyone who had left office to serve the Confederacy from holding office.

The fourth section ruled that no Confederate state could pay any debts it owed.

The Fourteenth Amendment presented a blunt challenge to the Confederate states. It forced them to either ratify it and join the Union or reject it and take their chances. Tennessee was the first Confederate state to ratify the amendment and rejoin the Union in 1866. By 1870, all states had ratified the amendment.

During this period, some former Rebel officers and soldiers organized a secret army to resist the Civil Rights Act and to support white control over African Americans. Supporters of civil rights were attacked by this group, which became known as the Ku Klux Klan.

The Ku Klux Klan spread terror and violence among those who supported civil rights.

Other Concerns

As if Johnson's problems with Congress were not enough, there were also many other issues to face. In his own family, Robert had gone back to heavy drinking, and he was a public embarrassment to the president. In the words of one visitor, "There is too much whiskey in the White House."

Johnson's brother, William, was killed in a hunting accident in October 1866. In addition, Eliza's continuing illness was so severe that she was barely even a presence in Washington, making only two public appearances during her time there. The Johnson's oldest daughter, Martha, assumed that role.

Internationally, Johnson faced trouble, as well. A group of Irishmen in the U.S. attempted to invade British North America (Canada) to support their homeland's independence. Because of U.S. treaties with England, Johnson was forced to stop these attacks. The Irish, however, tended to be loyal Democrats, and they withdrew their support of Johnson just as the Republicans abandoned him.

To the south, France had invaded Mexico and placed an emperor on the throne. Johnson faced mounting pressure to take direct action against the French. Although France had

A newspaper cartoon made fun of Seward's and Johnson's decision to buy Alaska from Russia.

violated the 1819 Monroe Doctrine against colonizing countries in North and South America, Johnson was not anxious to begin another war so soon after the Civil War.

Attorney General James Speed resigned to protest Johnson's actions.

Finally, in 1867, Johnson authorized Secretary of State William Seward to purchase Alaska—then called Russian America— from Russia for $7.2 million. This would eventually turn out to be among the best land purchases in American history. Newspapers at the time, however, called the move "Seward's Folly" and "Johnson's Polar Bear Garden."

Johnson's cabinet, which he had carried over from Lincoln, was split in its support of his policies. In July 1866, Attorney General James Speed, Postmaster General William Dennison, and Interior Secretary James Harlan all resigned to protest Johnson's Reconstruction policy. Secretary of War Edwin Stanton, another carryover, remained in his position but was outspoken about his differences with Johnson.

Replacing Stanton with a supporter of his polices became difficult for Johnson after Congress passed the Tenure of Office Act in 1867.

This act required Senate approval before the president could fire any official approved by the Senate, including the president's cabinet.

In part, the act was created to protect Stanton. The Tenure Act, however, also limited the president's role as commander-in-chief of the armed forces by requiring him to issue any orders through the commanding General of the Army. Johnson believed the act was unconstitutional and vetoed it, but the veto was easily overturned.

Secretary of War Edwin Stanton was a forceful opponent of Johnson.

At this point, Johnson once again tried to block the long-term plans of Congress. He replaced several Radical generals in charge of the South with more moderate leaders. He also deliberately misinterpreted parts of the Reconstruction Acts with the support of his new Attorney General Henry Stanberry. The boldest step Johnson took, however, was to remove his disloyal Secretary of War, Edwin Stanton.

Impeachment

Removing Stanton would accomplish two things for Johnson. First, it would get rid of his strongest opposition within his own cabinet. Stanton had consistently worked against Johnson's goals and, in several instances, had told Radical Republicans in Congress what Johnson was saying and planning in cabinet meetings. Second, Stanton's removal also directly challenged the Tenure of Office Act, which Johnson believed was unconstitutional. To achieve these gains, he was willing to risk even his political career.

The Constitution says that Congress can impeach—bring charges against—a president for "treason, bribery, or other high crimes and misdemeanors." If the House votes to impeach, the Senate holds a trial. If two-thirds of the Senate votes to convict, the president is removed from office.

★

Today, the cabinet position once known as Secretary of War is called the Secretary of Defense.

★

As Johnson and Congress became more bitterly divided, leaders of the Radical Republicans looked for ways to impeach him. On August 12, 1867, Andrew Johnson suspended Edwin Stanton from his duties and replaced him with war hero General Ulysses S. Grant. Stanton's reply to Johnson was a clear warning: "I am compelled (forced) to deny your right . . . without the advice and consent of the Senate and without any legal cause, to suspend me from office . . . I have no alternative but to submit, under protest."

Managers of the House impeachment included Senator Thaddeus Stevens, holding a cane.

When the Senate refused to confirm the change, General Grant gave the position back to Stanton. This move would ruin the relationship between Grant and Johnson for the rest of their lives. Grant felt that he had been used and dishonored by the President. He sent Johnson a note that read in part, "I cannot but regard this whole matter . . . as an attempt to involve me in the resistance of law . . . and thus to destroy my character before the country."

On February 21, 1868, Johnson sent notes to Stanton, the Senate, and General Lorenzo Thomas, informing them that Stanton was removed and Thomas would take his place. Stanton locked himself in his office, refusing to leave. Congress, meanwhile, convinced that Johnson's violation of the Tenure of Office Act qualified as a "high crime," made plans to impeach him.

Johnson recieves a summons to appear before the House of Representatives.

Representative Thaddeus Stevens led the movement. Stevens was a powerful figure who hated the South and all it stood for. His opponents said Stevens acted like someone who had been "raised on sour milk." After the war ended, Stevens, then seventy-five, promised to use his remaining years to make the South suffer. He had been an outspoken opponent of both Lincoln and Johnson for their Reconstruction plans.

Following Stevens' lead, the House voted to impeach Johnson by a count of 128-47. It marked the first time a president had ever been impeached. Johnson was charged with eleven different counts, most related to the removal of Stanton and appointment of Thomas. On March 30, 1868, Johnson's trial in the Senate began.

The High Court of Impeachment opened in March 1868.

★ In 1998, President Bill Clinton became the second U.S. president ever to have an impeachment trial. ★

Under the Constitution, a presidential impeachment trial is presided over by the Chief Justice of the Supreme Court—at that time, Salmon P. Chase. The Senate needed two-thirds of the members to vote for conviction on any one of the eleven charges. With fifty-four Senators voting, that meant thirty-six had to vote against Johnson. The president knew it would be close.

The men assigned to accuse Johnson included his political enemies, Congressman Stevens and Senator Butler. To defend him, Johnson chose former Supreme Court Justice Benjamin Robbin Curtis, a Republican, and Henry Stanberry, who resigned as attorney general to defend Johnson. Johnson did not appear at the trial.

The trial itself was not very interesting, except in a few dramatic moments. In his opening speech, Butler tried to tie Johnson to the assassination of Lincoln, an accusation that had never completely disappeared after the discovery of Booth's calling card in Johnson's hotel. "By murder most foul did he succeed to the Presidency, and is the elect of an assassin to that high office, and not of the people," declared Butler.

Most of the charges were very similar, so the Senate first focused on the eleventh article of impeachment, which summed them up. They added the charge that Johnson had denied the right of Congress to pass laws in states not fully represented in Congress.

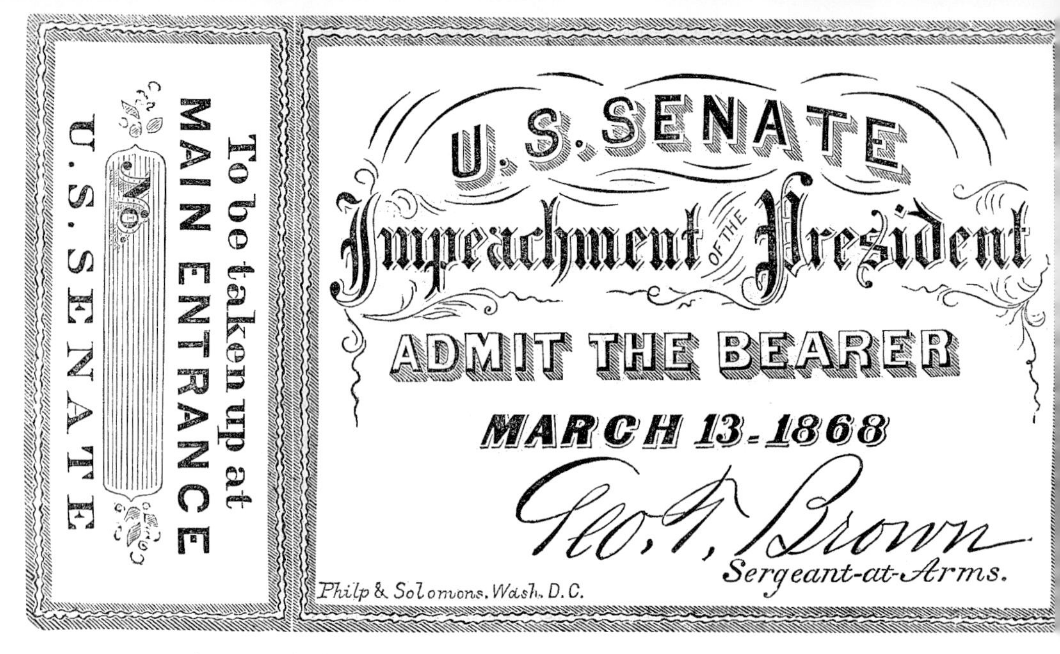

A ticket of admission to the impeachment trial.

Curtis and Stanberry focused on the fact that the accusations did not involve any "high crimes." The charges arose from differences of opinion, they claimed, and the right to express one's opinion was protected by the Constitution. Because Stanton had been appointed by Lincoln and not by Johnson, the Tenure of Office Act did not even apply to Stanton, argued Curtis.

Most Senators agreed with those points, but the question remained whether they would vote in Johnson's favor. Many were so anxious to remove the President that they did not particularly care about the charges. Johnson felt he could count on the nine Democrats and three conservative Republicans in the Senate. There were thirty Senators who Johnson assumed would move against him. That left twelve in the middle, and Johnson needed seven of those twelve Republican votes.

By early May, Justice Chase was ready to call for a vote. Johnson had tried to gain support from key senators. He agreed to appoint General John Schofield as new Secretary of War—a more acceptable nominee to Republicans than Thomas. He also promised not to interfere any longer with Reconstruction. On May 16, the Senate voted on the eleventh article. After one hour, the final count was thirty-five votes against Johnson, and nineteen votes for him. Andrew Johnson missed conviction by one vote.

General John Schofield became Secretary of War in 1868.

Ten days later, the second and third articles came up for a vote with the same result. The other eight articles were never voted on, and the trial was over. General Schofield replaced Secretary Stanton, and Johnson's presidency was saved. One cabinet member watched the president's reaction to the news:

> *He was calm, dignified, placid and self-possessed with no outward sign of agitation, whatever passions may have glowed in his breast. When the final result was announced, when we knew that the atrocity was ended . . . he received the congratulations of his Cabinet with the same serenity and self-possession which have characterized him throughout this terrible ordeal.*

The seven Republicans who had voted for Johnson did so at great personal expense. They were criticized by Senate colleagues, attacked by radical newspapers across the country, and attacked verbally—and physically—in their home states. Not one of the seven ever held public office again. Senator William Fessenden of Maine received the following note during the trial: "Any Republican Senator who votes against impeachment need never expect to get home alive."

On the other side, old Thaddeus Stevens never recovered from his anger at the outcome. "With all this great struggle of years in Washington, and the fearful sacrifice of life and treasure, I see little hope for the Republic." Complaining that his life had been a failure, Stevens died in November.

On His Way Out

Though it was only by one vote, Johnson's victory in the impeachment trial was an important moment for the nation. It was the first time a president had ever been impeached, and it was clear to most observers that the charges against Johnson were not "high crimes" as described by the Constitution. Instead, Johnson was put on trial because he opposed a powerful Congress who wanted to remove him because they disagreed with his acts. If the impeachment had ended with a conviction and Johnson's removal, that could have opened the door for a rule by Congress, thus overturning our system of checks and balances.

For Johnson, the victory was a sign of hope. With less than a year left in his term, he planned to use his success to gain his party's nomination for another term. Johnson had always been an excellent politician and a good reader of political signs. Unfortunately for him, those skills had failed him by 1868.

Johnson had returned to Washington as Lincoln's vice-president, supported by both Republicans and Democrats within the Union Party. Now, Republicans were set against him, and the Democrats considered him an embarrassment. Many Democrats also remained angry with Johnson for joining the Republican Lincoln in 1864. Even in Tennessee, his old associate, Parson Brownlow, worked to destroy the president's image at home. Ironically, Johnson's strongest supporters were now in the South, even though he had built his national career by standing so strongly against the secession.

★

In 1868, former Confederate General Robert E. Lee was the president of Virginia's Washington College, later renamed Washington and Lee.

★

That support was not enough. At the Democratic convention in July 1868, Johnson received less than one-third of the votes he needed for the nomination. Instead, Democrats chose New York Governor Horatio Seymour. In November, Seymour lost soundly to the Republican candidate, Ulysses Grant.

During Johnson's last months in office, Congress overturned every vetoed piece of legislation he sent them. Since most of his successes had been international, including the purchase of

President Johnson receives a delegation of Native Americans at the White House.

Alaska and the eventual withdrawal of French forces from Mexico without a fight, he made one more effort in that area. The United States had a series of outstanding conflicts with Great Britain, and Johnson sent a representative to England to work out a series of agreements.

Not surprisingly, the Senate refused to approve the resulting agreement. However, Johnson did manage to arrange a temporary truce with Indians in the West. Finally, on Christmas Day 1868, he pardoned all remaining Confederates, including Jefferson Davis who was still awaiting trial for his role as President of the Confederacy. Early in 1869, Johnson also pardoned the three men still in prison who had been convicted of playing a role in the assassination of Lincoln.

March 4, 1869 was Inauguration Day for the next president, Ulysses S. Grant. By tradition, the outgoing president usually attended the inauguration proceedings, but Johnson was still so bitter about Grant's disloyalty during the Stanton incident and impeachment that he refused to attend the ceremony. Instead, Johnson made one final speech to defend his actions. His only goals, he said, had been "to restore the Union of the States, faithfully to execute the office of President, and, to the best of my ability, preserve, protect, and defend the Constitution." With that final sentiment, Andrew Johnson went home to Tennessee.

★

President Grant, who took office after Johnson, smoked as many as twenty-five cigars per day. He died of throat cancer.

★

Chapter 6

"A LITTLE OF THE FIRE"

Despite his troubles in Washington, his enemies in both major political parties, and attacks by Parson Brownlow, Johnson returned home to Greeneville as a hero. In place of the banner which had read "Andrew Johnson, Traitor" in 1861, now stood a banner reading "Andrew Johnson, Patriot." Now sixty years old, Johnson was not sure what to do. Still a successful businessman, he put his financial affairs in order, then turned back to politics.

OPPOSITE: A photo of President Andrew Johnson, taken while he was in office.

A cartoon shows Horace Greeley, a newspaper publisher who ran against Grant in 1872.

Johnson still felt the need to prove that his views and actions in office had been correct. Winning a major election, he believed, would prove that people agreed with his stands and his ideals. In 1869, he ran for the U.S. Senate, but the state legislature failed to elect him by two votes. At the same time, tragedy again struck Johnson's family. Robert, who had never defeated his alcoholism, committed suicide.

After Washington, Greeneville seemed too small and quiet for him, but Eliza was there, and Martha and Mary and their families were nearby. Frank was finishing his studies at Georgetown College in Washington. In 1872, Johnson again made an attempt to return to national politics, by seeking election to the U.S. House of Representatives. He was also trying to build support for Democrat Horace Greeley, hoping that Greeley would defeat Grant. Both Greeley and Johnson were defeated. It was the second time in his life that Johnson lost a popular election.

In 1873, Johnson contracted cholera, and many thought he would die. On June 29, Johnson wrote what he believed was his final statement.

I have performed my duty to my God, my country, and my family—I have nothing to fear—approaching death to me is the mere shadow of God's protecting ring . . . here I will rest in quiet and peace beyond the reach of . . . envy and jealous enemies—where treason and traitors in state, backsliders and hypocrites in church can have no place.

Johnson did recover under Martha's good care, and he was more determined than ever to be elected to another public office.

That opportunity finally came in 1874. Johnson campaigned tirelessly for an open seat in the U. S. Senate, but his opponents were strong. In January of 1875, the state legislature began to vote for the Senate position; Johnson now had to win support of key Republicans. He did this by promising to be "moderate" in his policies, even promising not to oppose Grant "except in extreme cases." After fifty-four ballots, no candidate had won a majority of votes. Finally, on January 26, Johnson won the fifty-fifth ballot and was returned to the Senate at the age of 66. In a speech made during his campaign, Johnson said,

I know that when a man gets a little old, he is regarded as a cinder, something that won't generate any more heat, and he is thrown out on the ash pile . . . But, thank God, there is a little of the fire of youth running through my veins and in my heart yet.

Back to Washington

Johnson was the only president to serve in the Senate after his presidency. Given his relationship with the Senate seven years earlier, as well as his relationship with President Grant, many people wondered what his return would be like. Outside of Washington, Johnson's election was a sign of his recovered popularity.

★
By 1875, all Southern states had voted Reconstruction governments led by Radical Republicans from office.
★

On March 5, Johnson entered the Senate to be sworn in. Thirteen Senators who had voted to convict Johnson in his impeachment trial were still in office. This time, however, loud applause and a desk full of flowers greeted him. On March 20, Johnson rose to give what would turn out to be his last great speech.

Despite his promises not to oppose Grant, much of Johnson's speech attacked the president's policies. Johnson also described his commitment to protecting the Constitution, and when he finished, the chamber resounded with loud, enthusiastic applause. That applause must have been especially pleasing to Johnson, in the chamber where his political career had come within one vote of collapsing.

After that session, Johnson returned home. On July 28, he visited his daughter Mary at her home in Carter's Station, Tennessee. That night, he suffered a stroke, but, insisting he would be fine, he refused to allow Mary to send for a doctor. The next day, two doctors finally came and Martha was summoned. Johnson briefly appeared better, but on July 30, he suffered another stroke. This time he did not recover. At 2:30 A.M. on July 31, 1875, Andrew Johnson died. Though he had lived much of his life apart from his family, he died surrounded by Mary, Martha, and their families.

Johnson left specific instructions in the event of his death, and these were followed. His body was returned to Greeneville, laid in a casket, and wrapped in a large American flag, with a copy of the Constitution beneath his head. For the next four days, a steady stream of mourners came to pay their respects. In Washington, President Grant declared:

> *It becomes the painful duty of the president to announce to the people of the United States the death of Andrew Johnson . . . the varied nature and length of his public services, will cause him to be long remembered . . . (as) a distinguished public servant.*

Despite their mutual dislike, Grant ordered all departments of the government to be draped in black and all business stopped on August 3, the day of Johnson's funeral. Across the nation, newspapers again sang his praises. In the North, they wrote about his heroic loyalty to the Union during the Civil War. In the South, they described his services to protect Southern interests after the War.

Johnson in History

Andrew Johnson's place in history has been debated since his death. For a half-century after he died, historians focused on his failures as president. His impeachment highlighted his inability to work with Congress or to achieve a reasonable compromise on reconstructing the South. Despite Johnson's popularity at the end of his life, he was considered one of the least effective presidents in the nation's first century.

In the 1920s and 1930s, that opinion began to change. In 1926, in a case called Myers v. U.S., the Supreme Court finally struck down the Tenure of Office Act that had sparked Johnson's impeachment. This caused some key historians to re-examine Johnson's presidency. He was seen as a hero by some for his refusal to compromise and his willingness to oppose what he knew to be an illegal act of Congress.

★ Confederate President Jefferson Davis died at his home in Mississippi in 1889. ★

Then, in the 1960s, public opinion changed again. In that era, there was a focus on Civil Rights and the questions of equality between African Americans and white Americans, especially in the South. Andrew Johnson was criticized for allowing divisions between the races to continue by his refusal to force the South to treat freedmen equally.

In the end, Johnson was a product of both his time and his background. He never had a formal education and never traveled outside the South

The Civil Rights movements in the 1960s recalled the efforts of the late 1860s.

until he was an adult. He had no real family influence to guide his development, was married at 18, and spent most of his adult years away from his wife and children.

Johnson's political skills were beyond question. He was a brilliant debater and public speaker, and could be among the most convincing politicians of his time when he chose to be. Unfortunately, the devotion to duty that gained him the vice-presidency became his worst flaw as a president. He was unwilling to compromise with Congress, even though that refusal meant his plan of Reconstruction, partly devised by Abraham Lincoln, was not put into effect. His stubborn style also weakened the role of the president by forcing Congress to prove that it could override and outvote the President on major issues.

Most importantly, Johnson was unwilling to accept that the old ideas about slavery and the supremacy of the white race—ideas on which he had been raised—were wrong. While the actions of the Radical Republicans damaged the relations between the North and the South, Johnson's defense of the rights of the defeated whites at the expense of the freed slaves did even greater damage to relations between the races. Andrew Johnson's failure was not so much as a president or a politician, but in his inability to embrace the ideas his nation was just beginning to accept.

Glossary

assassinate to murder by sudden or secret attack

Carpetbagger a Northerner in the South after the American Civil War

compatriot a person born, residing, or holding citizenship in the same country as another

consumption a progressive wasting away of the body, especially from pulmonary tuberculosis

emancipate to free from restraint, control, or the power of another

impeach to remove from office

Ku Klux Klan a post-Civil War secret society advocating white supremacy

Manifest destiny a future event accepted as inevitable

nemesis a rival or opponent

pardon forgiveness of an offense without exacting a penalty

Reconstruction the reorganization and reestablishment of the seceded states in the Union after the American Civil War

Scalawag a white Southerner acting in support of the reconstructive governments after the American Civil War

secession formal withdrawal from an organization

treason the betrayal of a trust

typhoid fever a disease that causes fever, diarrhea, headache, and intestinal inflammation

veto to refuse to admit or approve

Whig a member or supporter of an American political party formed in 1834 in opposition to the Jacksonian Democrats, who were succeeded around 1854 by the Republican party

For More Information

Books

Malone, Mary. *Andrew Johnson.* Springfield, NJ: Enslow Publishers, Inc., 1999.

Nash, Howard P. *Andrew Johnson: Congress & Reconstruction.* Cranbury, NJ: Fairleigh Dickenson University Press, 2000.

Trefousse, Hans Louis. *Andrew Johnson: A Biography*. New York, NY: W.W. Norton & Company, 1997.

Trefousse, Hans Louis. *Impeachment of a President: Andrew Johnson, The Blacks, and Reconstruction.* Bronx, NY: Fordham University Press, 1999.

Welsbacher, Anne. *Andrew Johnson.* Minneapolis, MN: Abdo & Daughters, 2000.

Web sites

The Internet Public Library: Presidents of the United States
http://www.ipl.org/ref/POTUS/ajohnson.html
With information on the life and death of Andrew Johnson, including his personal and professional endeavors, this site also offers numerous links about Johnson and some of the important people he worked with.

Finding Precedent: The Impeachment of Andrew Johnson
http://www.impeach-andrewjohnson.com/
Harper's Weekly has launched this informative site, which offers information about the impeachment trial of President Andrew Johnson. It also has links to biographies, pictures, and histories of our seventeenth president.

National Park Service
http://www.nps.gov/anjo/
The Andrew Johnson National Historic Site has information for visitors, and includes links to other sites, including the Andrew Johnson Museum.

Index